DEALING WITH
YOUR PERSONAL CRISIS

DEALING WITH YOUR PERSONAL CRISIS

A formula for healing

Teo Babun

Dealing With Your Personal Crisis
A formula for healing
© 2004, Teo Bebun

ISBN 9780976501633

Unless otherwise indicated, Scripture quotations are taken
from the Holy Bible, New International Version®, NIV®.
Copyright© 1973, 1978, 1984 by International Bible Society.
Used by permission of Zondervan. All rights reserved.

Much of the inspirations of the author come from his
devotional times while using My Utmost For His Highest,
The Golden Book of Oswald Chambers, Discovery House
Publishers, Copyright© 1963. All rights reserved.

DEDICATION

To my wife Mary (Maija),

*who encouraged me and helped me
during my personal crisis.*

TABLE OF CONTENTS

PROLOGUE / 9

INTRODUCTION / 11

THE NEED FOR THE NEED
FOR A DAILY CRISIS PRAYER / 15

Step 1
**DEALING WITH THE QUESTION
"WHY DID THIS HAPPEN TO ME?" / 19**
- Because you are not of this world
- Because God wants you to know yourself

Step 2
GOD'S PROMISES TO PROVIDE AND RESTORE YOU / 25
- Allow Him to do what seems impossible to you
- God will order His angels to help you
- He promises to take care of all of your needs

Step 3
**DEALING WITH THE QUESTION
"WHAT SHOULD I BE DOING NOW?" / 33**
- Pray continually
- Worship God in words and music
- Commit yourself to do what pleases God
- Admit to God that you are a sinner
- Live only for Jesus
- Control yourself, act smart, and consult with Him before you act

Step 4
DIRECTIONS & WARNINGS- A ROADMAP
TO HELP YOU MAKE IMPORTANT DECISIONS / 49
- Be careful not to be tempted to solve the problem like a pagan
- Discern God's specific direction for you
- Don't be two faced or double minded
- Be obsessed by God
- Guard the state of your mind
- Be listening for His advice

Step 5
HOW YOU CAN BE CERTAIN
TO HEAR GOD'S DIRECTIONS / 65
- Let your spirit connect to the life of Jesus
- Ask God to reveal to you His "heart and mind"
- Meditate on His Word and listen for His soft voice

PROLOGUE

On May 23, 2003, at 4:00 P.M., I was called into my boss' office; he proceeded to accuse me of doing something I didn't do, and without any further discussion, he gave me the option to resign or be fired on the spot. I was hurt, in shock, and speechless. I was unemployed. I was in the midst of a crisis!

As I began to suffer through my personal crisis, I began to search for material that would help me deal with my pain. I was looking for a step-by-step process that would help me understand why this travesty and injustice happened to me, and what I needed to do to lessen my pain. Seeking guidance and wisdom, I searched the library for books on dealing with personal crisis, and talked to my closest friends, my family, and my pastor. Yet I found no relief. Some of them would even give me the type of advise that

I really didn't want to hear, like the famous clichÈ, "Well you know that nothing bad happens that doesn't bring something better"...or some variation of that.

I began to seek answers from the Bible, and I was inspired by God to find specific Scriptures that gave me comfort, guidance, direction, and warnings. I realized that God was placing before me a roadmap or "God-based guide" to help me deal with my perplexing hurt.

While meditating on God's Holy Scriptures, I became burdened with the thought that people are constantly in and out of crisis; or may know someone who is. Right there I decided to document my experience so that I could share my findings with others. My intention for publishing this guide is not to make my experience a principle for others; we must allow God to be as creative and original with you as He was with me. It is my hope and prayer that this Dealing with Your Personal Crisis-a formula for healing will be of some help to you as you seek God's direction and instructions on how to deal with your pain.

INTRODUCTION

> *"Father, through the calmness and control*
> *that you instill in me, I will demonstrate*
> *my confidence in you to take care of my needs.*
> *I confess to you that I know that in my life*
> *there is no such thing as chance.*
> *You ordain all of my circumstances."*

No one can ever be fully prepared for disaster or tragedy. But when tough times do arise, it's good to know that God has already anticipated our needs, and that He has provided, through the Holy Scriptures, a roadmap where we can turn to for a helping hand.

When stressful situations such as economic hardship, employment uncertainty, family or personal crisis come into our lives, God's Words will provide the healing formula to help rebuild our lives and ignite hope.

This guide is designed to help you and your families get through tough times together. It contains wisdom tips, quotes from Scripture, and suggested jump-start prayers to help you engage God; after which you can express your heart similarly to Him in your own words. Each chapter can help ease stress and help you plan for the future.

When times get tough, it is important to recognize that many unfamiliar things begin to happen to our minds and to our bodies. Here are some items taken from FEI Behavioral Health Employee Assistance and Crisis Management Programs, "The Critical Incident Response":

When times get tough

- Maintain as normal a schedule as possible, but don't overdo it; cut out unnecessary "busyness" and don't take on new projects
- Allow time for activities that make you happy
- Acknowledge that you may be operating below your normal level for a while
- Structure your time even more carefully than usual - it's normal to forget things when you're under stress
- Keep lists and double-check any important work
- Maintain control where you can - make small decisions even if you feel like the issue is unimportant, or you don't care (it is important to maintain control in some areas of your life)
- Spend time with others, even though it may be difficult

at first - it's easy to withdraw when you're hurt, but during this time you need the company of others
- Establish support systems with: family, friends, places of worship, school, coworkers, etc.
- Be aware that children are often unable to express their thoughts or feelings verbally; often they will act them out
- Let your children know that you are there to listen if they want to talk - be honest with them about your own thoughts and feelings
- Avoid self-prescribed medication and addictive substances like drugs, alcohol, caffeine, and nicotine - controlled substances may reduce the perception of stress, but they do not minimize anxiety
- If you feel as though you are alone and no one can help, don't let your feelings of panic, anger, and loneliness build, find help
- Recognize and deal with your stress - counseling or a support group can help
- Give yourself time - realize that you may feel better for a while, but later have a "relapse" (this is normal; allow plenty of time to adjust to the new realities you must face)

THE NEED FOR
A DAILY CRISIS PRAYER

While we are in the midst of a crisis, it is very important to start each morning with a prayer that encompasses the components of our hurt and our petitions to God. Normally, the body will feel broken, eyes will hurt, and we will feel somewhat sleepy; so it helps to have a "jump-start prayer" to help see Jesus clearly and get our energy and spiritual juices flowing.

The following prayer is only a suggestion. Perhaps it can be used as a starting point to a more profound personal prayer to the Lord:

> *"God, I seek Your wisdom. Help me not to let my problems choke Your Word out of me. Help me to trust You where I can not see. Help me not to be disloyal to You*

by choosing to take on the pressure of thinking and worrying about my problem. Prepare me for the times when You need to chastise me; please get my attitude ready so that my mind and my spirit will accept, at any cost, Your work in me to sanctify me. Help me pass the spiritual test when I come up against these things: injustice, meanness, discrimination, lies, ingratitude, and turmoil; above all, help me to remember that you demand that there be not even the slightest trace of resentment, even suppressed, in my heart, when I meet with tyranny and injustice.

"Lord, help me to do what is right, and not to act reckless so as to hurt my family or myself, or to embarrass You. Strengthen me so that no problem will affect my relationship with You in Jesus Christ. Help me to see clearly what You are teaching me through every problem that I face.

"Father, give me strength to have abandoned confidence in You. Protect me against self-pity, egocentrism, and self-blame. Sustain me during my tribulations. Help me to be alert to sin, and not to compromise one bit. Help me to draw from Your Grace constantly. Give me maturity to pray for those who are causing me

distress. I know that by Your providence, You bring me into all my circumstances and they are all spiritual in nature. Lord, I am aware that in my life there is no such thing as "chance".

"My King, show me Your will, and teach me to know how to pray and worship You in the midst of my trying circumstances. Right now, I place myself at the foot of Your Cross and give myself totally to You. Lord, make Your Grace abound in me. Help me to move to the other side of this so that healing can begin. Loving Father, lead me out of my exhaustion, and out of my condition of being half- dead. Penetrate me with Your spirit of life. Hold my hand; put me to bed; and sing me to sleep. Amen."

Step 1

DEALING WITH THE QUESTION "WHY DID THIS HAPPEN TO ME?"

Because you are not of this world

Remember that you are not of this world, and that's why the world hates you. Hate is the antithesis of love and it involves hostility. If the world persecuted Jesus, then it will also persecute you, because you belong to Christ. They will treat you this way because of His name, because they don't know God.

> *If the world hates you,*
> *keep in mind that it hated me first.*
> —JOHN 15:18

According to *Eerdmans' The New Bible Commentary: Revised*, the word, "world" here needs to be understood in the "moral sense of the world-order, under the control of adverse spiritual forces." Philip Yancey says that, "much of the suffering in our planet has come about because of two principles that God built into creation: a physical world that runs according to consistent natural laws, and human freedom." I found great relief in learning God's truths from these two theologians.

Perhaps like me, putting in perspective the characteristics of the "world" will help you understand the truth that: we live in this world, but we are not of it. We are like aliens in a world where the laws of nature (created by God) generate crisis; where humanity's free will (provided by God) generates crisis; and where the devil and his friends (allowed by God) are roaming around attacking every Christian they can find to create crisis in their lives.

JUMP-START PRAYER
Dear Lord, prepare my Heart and my mind, and give me power to face the rejection, persecution, and hate that I receive from

this world, because I am not of this world-I belong to You. Abba, strengthen me and give me wisdom to know how to walk and act in the midst of the attacks and the injustice. Instill in me pride in my relationship with you; I desire to have others see Christ in me. Lord, I choose You and not the things of this world!

▶▶| Add now your own personal prayer.

WHERE TO FIND ADDITIONAL HELP:
Luke 13:10-16; Psalm 71:14-24.

Because God wants you to know yourself

Make an effort to know yourself. God knows exactly your character and your possibilities. He knows what you are capable of doing and your potential-He knows your heart. Jesus led the Apostle Peter from one crisis to the next until he was able to know himself.

> *Then Jesus replied, "Have I not chosen you, the Twelve? Yet one of you is a devil!"*
> —JOHN 6:70

I once heard a Catholic priest from New Orleans say that, "in this life, pain is inevitable, but desperation is optional." The priest was right on! After all, we live in an imperfect world with imperfect people and imperfect systems. There is no such thing as a panacea world. The only question is when and where we will experience hurt, disappointment, injustices, and everything else we associate with the "pain of life". It is one of God's ways to help us find and understand ourselves.

The fact is that we are human. We can not find or understand ourselves through success, because we lose our head over pride. And we can not understand or accept ourselves through the monotony of our daily life because we give in to complaining. The question then is how are we to act when we experience pain? What kind of conduct will we manifest when we are in the midst of our personal crisis? and will we allow God's work to be displayed in our lives?

Desperation is only an option for those that have no hope, but we have perfect hope in Jesus Christ!

JUMP-START PRAYER:
God, help me to realize Your purpose in the difficulties and troubles that come into my life. Father, in spite of all these fires of

sorrow, protect me so that I may remain the person that You created me to be. Jesus, I accept that You allow: sorrows, difficulties, sufferings, and tribulations into my life, to help me find and understand myself better. God, in the midst of all my difficulties protect my attitude, and keep me from destroying myself. Gracious God, give me wisdom and maturity. Jesus, help me to learn what You want me to be, reveal the true me, and help me to live like you!

▶▶| **Add now your own personal prayer.**

WHERE TO FIND ADDITIONAL HELP:
Proverbs 3:5-6; John 12:27-29; John 16:33.

STEP 2

GOD'S PROMISE TO PROVIDE AND RESTORE YOU

Allow Him to do what seems impossible to you

Ask Him to place His hand upon you, so that He may give you total peace, support, comfort, and strength. Recognize that if you are in despair and in a state of helplessness, there is nothing humanly possible that can be done. Do not be afraid, just allow Him to do what seems impossible to you; watch Him provide and reveal Himself in His awesome majesty.

> *When I saw him, I fell at his feet as though dead.
> Then he placed his right hand on me and said: "Do not be
> afraid. I am the First and the Last. I am the Living One;
> I was dead, and behold I am alive for ever and ever!
> And I hold the keys of death and Hades.*
> —REVELATION 1:17, 18

According to the movie *Lagaan*, a village in the heart of India became famous when a group of farmers believed that their god could create a miracle and help them do what seemed impossible by defeating a team of British officers in a game of Cricket. Losing the game would have resulted in the farming villagers paying twice their normal tax to the British authorities. They believed that their god would help them. Then they did a remarkable thing and beat the British.

As Christians, we believe that our God can and will act directly to give us support and comfort. He promises to clothe us in righteousness and to give us the roadmap that we need to follow Him for peace and strength. He will use all the tools that He has at His disposal through: His nature, His Word, other people, our heart, and so many other ways. We only need to "allow" Him to do it.

Casting, in fly fishing, means the continued throwing of the fish bate over the water. The Apostle Peter, in 1 Peter 5:7 wrote, "Cast all your anxiety on him because he cares for you." Peter was certain that God's love and concern for us was so complete that we can continue to direct to Him all of our emotions and mental apprehensions...and He will take care of them. The issue then is our relationship with God established by faith, but this faith is not a vague or a general feeling. It is belief, acceptance, and trust directed toward God in Jesus Christ.

JUMP-START PRAYER:
Abba, you are my hope; you won't allow me to despair. Help me Lord to walk by faith and to trust you. Protect me dear God, from the demon of hopelessness; it is from the pit of hell. Strengthen me by placing your right hand upon me and give me total peace and comfort. Jehovah, you hold the keys of death and Hades; you can do what seems humanly impossible. Living God, help me not to be afraid or to despair while I am waiting for you to reveal yourself through your miracles. Oh God, hear my prayers!

▶▶ **Add now your own personal prayer.**

WHERE TO FIND ADDITIONAL HELP:
Psalm 31:3; John1:1-3; Joshua 1:9; Psalm 23:2.

God will order His angels to help you

Be certain and confident that God will lift you up so that you will not trip or fall. He will restore you and He will always be with you. God will command His angels to guard your ways, because He is The God of love and peace.

> *Then no harm will befall you, no disaster will come near your tent. For he will command his angels concerning you to guard you in all your ways; they will lift you up in their hands, so that you will not strike your foot against a stone.*
> —PSALM 91:10-12

In his book *Angels*, evangelist Billy Graham says that an angel is a "heavenly being charged by God with some commission." Thirty-four books of the Bible make reference to angels. Angels are termed "ministering spirits" in Hebrews 1:14. They have been duly commissioned and sent forth with responsibility of aiding believers. Angels protect humans from physical harm to those that seek refuge in the Lord (Ps. 91:11-13). They released the apostles from prison (Acts 5:19), and Peter from prison (Acts 12:7-11).

I don't know about you, but I find great relief in knowing with certainty, that God has created this army of extraterrestrial visitors to guard us in all of our ways. To guard us means to take precautions in order to avoid some unwanted consequences, and to watch over or to shield us from danger.

We can choose to believe God's Holy Bible and its promises, or we can choose not to believe, or even to ignore the truth. As for me, I have chosen to rejoice on God's promise that He will command His angels to shield me from danger. I will give praises to our Lord for this gift, and I will take advantage of this privilege in my prayers, by reminding God that I am in need of His guarding angels today, more than ever.

JUMP-START PRAYER:
Dear God, protect my heart so that it will not break with the difficulties that I face. Protect my mind from worrying about my problems, and protect my spirit against the temptations that I face. Oh Father, command Your angels to guard my ways and to lift me up in their hands so that I will not trip over the rocks, nor be caught in the traps. Lord, give me firm and certain confidence to know that You will restore me. Oh God, You are my fortress and my song!

▶▶| **Add now your own personal prayer.**

WHERE TO FIND ADDITIONAL HELP:
Matthew 4:6; Matthew 13:41; Luke 4:10; Hebrews 1:14.

He promises to take care of all of your needs

Be confident and courageous, because man can do nothing to you that the Lord has not allowed. Look around and be aware of God's assurances to you. He promises to be with you always, and to take care of all of your needs.

> *So we say with confidence,*
> *"The Lord is my helper; I will not be afraid.*
> *What can man do to me?"*
> —HEBREWS 13:6

I met Pepe Bretones in Hartford, CT. Pepe was a Cuban refugee working for minimum wages as a maintenance man in a tool shop. In 1962, he had escaped the communist regime of Fidel Castro with his wife and his eight year old son, and thirteen year old daughter. In Cuba, Pepe had been a wealthy and well-known trader of garments and fine linens.

When I talked to Pepe about his "misfortune", he would always say that he was thankful that the Lord had saved his family from socialism, and humbled by the joy that he had brought to the Lord. It took me a while to understand what this good man meant. When God gives to us, or provides for us, it gives Him great joy too, because God loves to give to us to meet our needs.

I believe that's what Jesus had in mind in Matthew 6:25 when He said, "Therefore I tell you, do not worry about your life, what you will eat or drink; or about your body, what you will wear. Is not life more important than food, and the body more important than clothes?", and then he adds, "So do not worry, saying, 'What shall we eat?' or "What shall we drink?" or "What shall we wear?" For the pagans run after all these things, and your heavenly Father knows that you need them. But seek first his kingdom and his righteousness, and all these things will be given to you as well."

JUMP-START PRAYER:
My Abba, blessed is Your name Oh Lord! And be exalted above the heavens; let Your glory be all over the earth. My God, I will not be afraid of anything that man can do to me because You are my Lord and my helper. You promise to take care of all of my needs; You will do all that You say in Your time. Father, give me courage and make me stronger in my faith by being aware of Your assurances and of Your miracles. I will not fear because You said that You will never leave me. You are my stronghold

and my song. God, even as I think of my lowest and most desperate moments and situations, I now realize that You never left me; You were always with me even as You have promised. Lord, I will only look to You for justice; seeking justice in this world will only lead me to complain, and to indulge myself in self-pity. You are my helper. Man has done nothing to me that You have not allowed. I will trust in You!

▶▶ **Add now your own personal prayer.**

WHERE TO FIND ADDITIONAL HELP:
Psalm 109:26-31; Psalm 38:21-22; Jeremiah 1:8.

STEP 3

DEALING WITH THE QUESTION: "WHAT SHOULD I BE DOING NOW?"

Pray continually

Pray continually. Make it as common as breathing, and be completely certain that prayer is always answered. God will answer your prayers in the best way-every time!

> *Pray continually.*
> —1 THESSALONIANS 5:17

As Christians, the one thing that we are called to do in this life is to pray for those we come in contact with, such as our friends and our family. The theologian, Oswald Chambers said, "If you are not receiving the "hundredfold" which Jesus promised, and not getting insight into God's Word; then start to pray for your friends-enter into the ministry of the inner life."

How can a non-believer understand that if we want our prayers answered, then all we have to do is to pray for others? It may seem crazy or foolish, but if we believe in what God tells us in His Bible, then it is totally true. The author of the book of Job in 42:10 says, "after Job had prayed for his friends, the Lord made him prosperous again and gave him twice as much as he had before." Go figure!

JUMP-START PRAYER:
My Abba and my King, help me to think of prayer as necessary and as common as the breath in my lungs and the blood from my heart. Help me to pray in all occasions; continuously, and without ceasing. Lord, help me to get even a small understanding of the importance of praying for others. Provide me with the necessary maturity to set aside my personal needs and demands, so that I can pour my life out in the work of intercession. Father, help me also to have total certainty: that You are listening, that You understand, and that You will respond every time. And Lord, help me to look forward in great anticipation to how You will answer my prayer!

▶▶| **Add now your own personal prayer.**

WHERE TO FIND ADDITIONAL HELP:
Matthew 19:29; Job 42:10.

Worship God in words and music

Worship God with all your heart and with all your soul. Worship Him in music. Worship Him in private and in public. Worship Him in the light and in the darkness. Worship Him because He is a great God!

> *Come, let us sing for joy to the LORD;*
> *let us shout aloud to the Rock of our salvation.*
> *For the LORD is the great God,*
> *the great King above all gods.*
> —PSALM 95:1, 3

The Reverend Fernando Lamigueiro, a retired founder of a number of ministries and mission work throughout the Caribbean, once told me to consider the significance of worship:

It is obedience to a divine command.
It is a means of nourishing the spirit.
It assists in achieving spiritual growth.
It encourages others in their spiritual development.
It shows the world where my priorities are.
It is one means of expressing my love for God.
It is an avenue God has provided by which I can praise His name.

> It is the offering of spiritual sacrifices.
> It is a way of showing my thanksgiving to God for all He has done for me.
> It is a period of communion with God with the world shut out entirely.
> It is an experience that should make the heart of every Christian glad.

While in the midst of my personal crisis, nothing gave me more peace than listening to worship music and nothing gave me more comfort than worshiping God with other Christians. In any event, worship that is accepted by God is a privilege that is unique to the Christian. It is not a right, so we should take advantage of this special gift.

Our God is an awesome God! He is worthy to be worshipped and praised! What a deal we have!

Jump-Start Prayer:
Praise You Father, Lord of the universe! You always do what You say; You defend the wronged; You feed the hungry; and You lift me up when I fall. My Lord, You are great, You have limitless strength; You push the wicked into the ditch. Hallelujah! Praise Yahweh from heaven, praise Him from the mountaintops. Let every living, breathing creature praise Yahweh! My deliverer! Hallelujah!

▶▶ Add now your own personal prayer.

Where to find additional help:
1 Peter 2:5; Psalm 96:6; Psalm. 146:1; Ephesians 5:19.

Commit yourself to do what pleases God

Be determined to do what pleases God. Commit to Him that you will obey His commandments and His teachings. Openly declare that you will be faithful to the Lord, and that you have absolute confidence in His plans and His wisdom.

> *Dear friends, if our hearts do not condemn us,*
> *we have confidence before God*
> —1 John 3:21

Jesus said to His followers, "If you love Me, keep My commandments." It's useless to talk about loving Jesus if we do not obey Him. The proof of our love for Jesus lies squarely in our obedience to Him. The way to commit ourselves to do what pleases God is to do what He asks us to do. If we can keep the commandments of God, we will prove to the world; we will prove to the Heavenly Father;

and we will prove to Jesus, that we love Him. It's just that simple. We just need to look for practical ways to work that out in our lives.

Have you seen the bumper sticker that says, "Honk if you love Jesus"? I haven't seen one of those for a long time. I did see one that says, "Tithe if you love Jesus. Any idiot can honk". Well is true, anybody can honk; but if we love Jesus, we need to prove it. We need to show Him that we love Him. Keep His commandments; that's the way He will know that we're doing what pleases Him.

I am convinced that if we do what pleases God, we will develop faith in Him. Faith is confidence in the righteous character of God that fosters truth and hope, even when the evidence fosters doubt and despair. Job was a man who feared God. In the Old Testament context this refers to a man who had a reverential truth in God coupled with a hatred for evil. "The fear of the Lord is the beginning of wisdom" (Psalm 111:10; Proverbs 9:10). With that type of trust in God, our sensitivity and hatred of sin will grow everyday.

JUMP-START PRAYER:
Lord, help me to have the discipline to do only what pleases You, as I follow Your commandments and Your teachings with total

confidence. Jehovah, instill in me a desire to obey Your directions and precepts. Father, I want to rely on You for everything. Not on my capabilities, or my knowledge, or anything else. Lord, I commit today to do what pleases You, to obey You, to believe in You, and to have a disciplined life. Precious God, I will be loyal, I will obey You, I will serve You, and I will be faithful today!

▶▶| **Add now your own personal prayer.**

WHERE TO FIND ADDITIONAL HELP:
Proverbs 4:23; John 15:14; Colossians 1:12-14.

Admit to God that you are a sinner

Admit to God that as a human being you have an inclination to sin. Bring yourself mentally to terms with the fact that sin is in this world. Sin makes the foundation of your thinking: unpredictable, uncontrollable, and irrational. It is the explanation of the grief and sorrow of life, and it is the explanation of why Jesus Christ came to earth. Recognize your sins before Him, and ask Him for forgiveness, as this will be the sign that your spirit is at work and that your face has been turned towards God.

> *We have sinned and done wrong.*
> *We have been wicked and have rebelled;*
> *we have turned away from your commands and laws.*
> —Daniel 9:5

When I first read Daniel 9:5, I was stunned, because the Bible is very pronounced in denying that all suffering results from specific sins. The more I meditated on God's Word, the more I realized that the message was not that I should attribute my crisis to any specific sin, nor that I should see my pain as some type of punishment for a human mistake. On the contrary, God was teaching me that He wanted me to be totally dependent on Him; to pray in the spirit, and not in the flesh. For me to do that, I needed to admit and recognize before Him that I was a sinner.

We all sin and break our fellowship with God; therefore, we need to experience God's forgiveness for both our actions and our attitudes.

Even though our relationship with God is permanent and we are totally forgiven, we still need to deal with our sins on a day-to-day basis in order to experience continuing fellowship with Him.

We must be careful not to fall in the trap of condemning ourselves. Jesus spent His days on earth healing diseases and not causing them. Christ died for our sins. The lesson then is very simple: To approach Him in spirit and truth, we must acknowledge to Him our sinful nature.

JUMP-START PRAYER:
Father, help me to be alert to the fact of sin and the subtle ways that I can be attacked, and tempted by the evil one. I confess to You that in my weakness, I often fall in the traps of Satan. Lord, alert me to the danger signs, and remind me of the disasters that sin can bring into my life. Strengthen me God, so I won't compromise in anything, not even one bit. Give me fortitude to walk away from the settings that can tempt me to fall. Precious Jesus, forgive me for the times that I have offended You. My wish is to obey You in everything. Protect me with the redeeming blood of Jesus Christ against the attacks of the Devil and his demons. Gracious Father, hear my prayer; I pray for the Holy Spirit to intercede on my behalf. Praise You Lord for Your mercy, for understanding my isolation, and for loving me unconditionally!

▶▶| **Add now your own personal prayer.**

WHERE TO FIND ADDITIONAL HELP:
Isaiah 53:3; Luke 22:53; 1 Peter 3:18.

Live only for Jesus

Be a true disciple to Jesus. Be passionately devoted to Him. Living for Jesus is the most exciting thing that you can do. It is the beginning of a life of adventure with an all-loving, all-powerful God. Ask the Holy Spirit to help you love and glorify Him. And live only for one thing: Jesus! Always Jesus! Only Jesus! Jesus in everything!

> *"Simon, Simon, Satan has asked to sift you as wheat."*
> —LUKE 22:31

The first step in getting to our goal of being filled with the fullness of God is allowing Christ to dwell in our heart. The word "dwell" means to inhabit, it means to take up residence. We are inviting Jesus Christ to come into our lives, into our hearts, and to be there 24 hours a day, seven days a week. But how can Christ live in us?

Colossians 1:27 refers to "Christ in you, the hope of glory." This is possible because Colossians 3:3 says, "For you died, and your life is now hidden with Christ in God." So we are hidden in God, and God the Holy Spirit is in us. This means to me that Jesus Christ hides us in God the Father and indwells us by God the Holy Spirit.

Dealing With Your Personal Crisis /43

We get confirmation to this in John 14:16-18, "And I will ask the Father, and he will give you another Counselor to be with you forever— the Spirit of truth. The world cannot accept him, because it neither sees him nor knows him. But you know him, for he lives with you and will be in you. I will not leave you as orphans; I will come to you."

When we trust Jesus to be our Savior, we can have confidence in our relationship with Him because we have been completely forgiven and accepted by God. Only Christ's death on the Cross is sufficient to provide this proper relationship with God. When we spend time in God's Word, we can achieve our objective of being filled by the fullness of God. Christ will dwell in our hearts, we will begin to comprehend the truth, and we will begin to know the love of Christ. Then we can begin to live only for Jesus!

JUMP-START PRAYER:
My Jesus, I want to have a personal relationship and passionate devotion to You; I want for everything that I do to be motivated by my love for You. Come into my life Lord Jesus and live in my heart. Jesus, help me to live only for You: imitating You in everything that I do and say, anticipating what You would do in any situation, and always trying to make You proud of me. Oh Holy Spirit of God, set my soul on fire with love and devotion

for Jesus Christ. May everything that I do and say glorify my Savior!

▶▶ **Add now your own personal prayer.**

WHERE TO FIND ADDITIONAL HELP:
Ephesians 3:17-19; Nehemiah 8:10; John 14:9.

Control yourself, act smart, and consult with Him before you act

Prepare your mind for action. Allow Jesus to examine your heart in the midst of your crisis and difficulties. Stay strong, focused and patient, while the Lord prepares the way and gets you in shape. Be self-controlled, and place your hope totally in the Grace of Jesus Christ. Seek wisdom from Him. Often, the only way to know if Jesus has given you a pure heart is to go through difficult crisis and sufferings.

> *Trying to find out the time and circumstances to which the Spirit of Christ in them was pointing when he predicted the sufferings of Christ and the glories that would follow.*

Dealing With Your Personal Crisis / 45

> *Therefore, prepare your minds for action;*
> *be self-controlled; set your hope fully on the grace*
> *to be given you when Jesus Christ is revealed.*
> **—1 Peter 1:11,13**

We're hurting, and we're heartbroken. Prolonged pain is brutal. In the midst of our pain we begin to lose our self-esteem. Not falling into a depression requires a lot of persistence, and persistence requires energy. Heartbreak can dredge up feelings of grief, anger, betrayal, bitterness, and regret. Those feelings are normal, but the trick is figuring out how to move on.

I found during my crisis that it was important to build an interim structure to my day, in order to replace the old pattern of work. I discovered that the brain functions best when there's structure. I made a schedule that I honored every day. I got up at a regular hour, got dressed, exercised, got adequate sleep, and kept a journal.

The journal was particularly important as a way of dealing with the emotional upheaval of the change in my life. It gave me a place to vent, with no judgment about what I was saying or feeling, and it allowed me to process my experience. Finally, it gave me a great list of emotions to place at the foot of the Cross of Christ. I never lacked for specific prayer requests, and never acted before asking Jesus for His direction. I suggest writing early in the morning to capture dream fragments, hopes, and fears.

Humanly speaking, it takes time to recover from such feelings-to get over the shock and disorientation and to process our new circumstances. But we must remember that, "we are not of this world". So starting now, we need to get off the couch, act with intelligence, and start letting Jesus do His thing in us!

Jump-Start Prayer:
My Abba and my King, search my heart and examine my mind, see if there is any dark spot that needs to be removed, and set me free. Strengthen me to allow You to shape me and mold me as You are getting ready to make Your vision real in me, and preparing me for action. Lord, create in me a pure heart and a new spirit so that I can be totally committed and obedient to You. Father, in the midst of my difficulties, make me able to act smart, be self-controlled, and make you proud of my conduct. God, I seek your counsel in all of my actions.

▶▶ Add now your own personal prayer.

Where to find additional help:
Matthew 5:41; Matthew 7:11; Genesis 41:40.

STEP 4

DIRECTIONS & WARNINGS: A ROAD-MAP TO HELP YOU MAKE IMPORTANT DECISIONS

Be careful not to be tempted to solve the problem like a pagan

Be careful not to act like the pagans in a crisis. Be daring enough to invest yourself in the character of God to bring honor to Him. Be aware that God may ask you to do something which is totally against your common sense. If He does, don't hold back. He may want you to risk everything for Him!

> *Still another said, "I will follow you, Lord;*
> *but first let me go back and say good bye to my family."*
> —LUKE 9:61

When a crisis comes, we feel that we have no control over the event itself, but we still have some control over our responses. We can lash out in hostility and rage against the injustice of life that has deprived us of peace, or we can look for good in unexpected sources. For example, as I studied the Bible, I was convinced that I needed to be on my knees praying for my apparent enemies, and thanking God for all His blessings. After all, we are the children of God!

Look what is written in Philippians 2:14-16, "Do everything without complaining or arguing, so that you may become blameless and pure, children of God without fault in a crooked and depraved generation, in which you shine like stars in the universe as you hold out the word of life—in order that I may boast on the day of Christ that I did not run or labor for nothing."

JUMP-START PRAYER:
My Abba and my King, I was trained from the time that I was born to be self-reliant, to solve my own problems, and to use my

common sense. In a crisis, I was taught to pursue justice in my own terms. Father, guide me in my efforts to solve a wrong that has been done to me. Protect me against acting or using tactics that are used by the pagans. Lord, teach me how to: invest in Your character, obey you blindly, and risk everything for You. Jehovah, I place my total trust in you, and will rely in the examples, models, and promises that You give me in Your Word. God, help me to have spiritual ears to hear You clearly when You speak to me.

▶▶| Add now your own personal prayer.

WHERE TO FIND ADDITIONAL HELP:
Job 2:4-7; Matthew 6:25.

Discern God's specific direction for you

In the midst of your crisis, be alert to God's direction for you; be determined to do His will, and then be careful to obey Him. Don't offend God by double-checking with other people's opinions; their heart is not God's heart. God is absolutely right, so place your total trust in Him. God's objective is that His Son might be manifested in Your mortal flesh.

Babun

> *But Jesus would not entrust himself to them, for he knew all men. He did not need man's testimony about man, for he knew what was in a man.*
> —JOHN 2:24, 25

Sometimes, I get really frustrated by my Christian friends and family who seem to have a "pad" answer for every one of my feelings. They have an inadequate view of our crisis, yet they have lots of answers. The two most common responses seem to be: "you must have done something wrong", and "you must have not been praying hard enough". Other quick comments were: "it is a warning from God", "it's your stubborn rebellion", and "sin is in your life". Although their comments are usually well-intentioned, they are only human opinions.

Sheldon Vanauken is attributed to have said that "the best argument for Christianity is Christians: their joy, their certainty, their completeness. But the strongest argument against Christianity is also Christians-when they are somber and joyless, when they are self-righteous and smug in complacent consecration, when they are narrow and repressive, then Christianity dies a thousand deaths." This statement supports that "man", whether Christian or not, is simply "man", and must think and feel like "man".

Dealing With Your Personal Crisis /51

On the other hand, Jesus showed that He had the heart of God when, after healing a blind man, He said, "this happened so that the work of God might be displayed in his life."

I don't know about you, but this is enough warning for me to decide to get my direction from Jesus and not from any man.

JUMP-START PRAYER:
My Abba and my King, thank You for loving me so much that You set aside everything to take care of me. Help me to be transformed spiritually by discerning what is in Your heart, and receive Your direction. Teach me to trust You completely because You are always absolutely right. Protect me against my inclination to trust the wisdom of human beings, only to be later very disappointed and disillusioned because their objectives and their goals are not the same as Yours. Bless you Lord, for your desire for me is that I might manifest Jesus in my mortal flesh!

▶▶| **Add now your own personal prayer.**

WHERE TO FIND ADDITIONAL HELP:
John 17:21; John 13:17; Matthew 18:5; Hebrews 109.

Don't be two faced or double minded

Be careful not to be a hypocrite and a traitor to Jesus. Don't be a "double minded person", as was Judas. Don't get spiritually lazy. You must be ready and prepared to face your crisis with consistency and integrity.

> *Whoever believes in him is not condemned,*
> *but whoever does not believe stands condemned already*
> *because he has not believed in the name of God's one*
> *and only Son. This is the verdict: Light has come into*
> *the world, but men loved darkness instead of light*
> *because their deeds were evil.*
> —John 3:18, 19

Who wants to be a hypocrite and a traitor to Jesus? We will if we are a person who one moment is thanking God for His wonderful protection, provision, and plans, while the next moment, we are vacillating, hesitating, and uncertain about everything. Or if one moment we are praising God and singing His praises, while the next moment, we are shaking our fists in the air, and complaining about every single thing. David said about these kinds of people in Psalm 119:113, "I hate double-minded men, but I love your law", and James said in James 1: 8, "he is a double-minded man, unstable in all he does." Certainly, being a double-minded person is not a good thing. A person with integrity is not divided. That's duplicity or merely pretending, and that is hypocrisy.

When you make a list of people in the Bible who modeled integrity, Joseph has to be on the top of that list. Joseph lived a life of integrity and honor before the Lord. In the worst of times, he trusted God to work out the results, and in the best of times, he acknowledged that every privilege comes from the Lord's hand. Joseph's integrity was tied to God's sovereignty. Joseph believed that God was sovereign, and that God was faithful; so he did what was right, trusting God for the outcome. Joseph's life provides us with a model for living-out integrity each day.

We must constantly demonstrate our honesty, because that is the way that God wants us to live, not just to pass a test that somebody else may be writing or constructing for us.

JUMP-START PRAYER:
Blessed Father, my desire is to be totally honest with You and with my fellow men. Cleanse me of any tendency that I may have to be a traitor to You, by talking as a Christian, but acting

as a Judas. Energize me to do what is right always, so that I am ready to deal with the rough road of life; things such as: turmoil, injustice, ingratitude, and degradation. Lord, I want to serve You with a clean conscience and a grateful heart. Thank You that Your Grace is sufficient!

▶▶| Add now your own personal prayer.

WHERE TO FIND ADDITIONAL HELP:
Romans 8:7; John 15:14; Luke 16:15; John 9:8.

Be obsessed by God

Be obsessed by God, then nothing else will be able to take over your life; not concerns, nor problems, nor worries. Worrying is unbelief in Him. How can you worry if you believe that He is all knowing, all powerful, all loving, and that He totally surrounds you? Let your vision of God be one of majesty, power and might. Let Him purify You through the circumstances and ordeals that He brings into Your life.

> *Who, then, is the man that fears the LORD?*
> *He will instruct him in the way chosen for him.*
> —PSALM 25:12

To be obsessed by something is to be influenced or controlled by a powerful force. In the midst of our crisis, we must be controlled by God, and not by our strong emotions. To do that , we must be constantly aware of God's presence. And to develop such a state of mind, we must totally surrender to Christ. In other words, we must abide in Jesus Christ.

Nothing brings this message home more clearly than Jesus' own words from John 15:4-8*, "Abide in me, and I will abide in you. No branch can bear fruit by itself; it must abide in the vine. Neither can you bear fruit unless you abide in me. I am the vine; you are the branches. If a man abides in me and I in him, he will bear much fruit; apart from me you can do nothing...If you abide in me and my words abide in you, ask whatever you wish, and it will be given you. This is to my Father's glory, that you bear much fruit, showing yourselves to be my disciples."

JUMP-START PRAYER:
My Abba and my King, how can I be so absolutely unbelieving with worrying when I know that You totally surround me? Forgive me for offending You with my unbelief. Help me to look

---

* Note that I took the liberty of changing "remain" to "abide" in the NIV translation.

to You in everything, and to help create a spiritual wall against the assaults of the enemy and the tribulations of this world. Lord, thank You for Your promise to be my shelter. Nothing, but absolutely nothing, can break through Your shelter of protection for me. All I have to do is to spend time with You and abide in You. Loving Father help me to be strong, and not afraid of Your cleansing process. Yahweh, You are all powerful and all mighty; You know all things. Lord, in all the world there is no one like You. You are the Alfa and the Omega-You know what You are doing!

▶▶| **Add now your own personal prayer.**

WHERE TO FIND ADDITIONAL HELP:
Matthew 11:25; Matthew 6:30; Matthew 6:25.

Guard the state of your mind

Be aware that at a time of crisis, you are spiritually distracted instead of spiritually self-controlled. Be careful and guarded about the state of your mind. Do not conform to the pattern and counterfeits of this world. Do not confuse your zeal and enthusiasm for discernment. God wants you to be something that you have never been before.

Dealing With Your Personal Crisis / 57

> *Therefore, I urge you, brothers, in view of God's mercy,*
> *to offer your bodies as living sacrifices, holy and pleasing*
> *to God—this is your spiritual act of worship.*
> *Do not conform any longer to the pattern of this world,*
> *but be transformed by the renewing of your mind.*
> *Then you will be able to test and approve*
> *what God's will is—his good, pleasing and perfect will.*
> —ROMANS 12:1, 2

At the onset of my crisis, I had no idea how difficult it would be for me to concentrate, or to think clearly. It was like my mind wanted to continuously go back to the period before the crisis started, to avoid dealing with the realities that I was facing. I realized that I had become vulnerable to all types of mental and spiritual distractions, but I didn't know how to protect myself, or have the energy to do so.

The morning after my crisis started, my dear wife, Mary, suggested that I begin walking with her every morning for 40 minutes. Mary must have been inspired by the Holy Spirit! That little walk not only produced much needed oxygen for my brain, lungs, and vital organs, but also became a critical time away from the "doldrums" of my crisis. Our daily walk became a time to look at my crisis from a distance; like looking at the forest instead of the trees. Soon I began to value our walk for other reasons: it gave me a scheduled time to talk with Mary, it helped me to refresh my mind, and it energized me.

I am thankful that Mary encouraged me to start walking. Like me, you need to find a way to protect yourself from the mental weakness, and the handicaps that are introduced into our lives when we enter a period of personal crisis.

JUMP-START PRAYER:
My Abba and my King, I recognize that my life is not now, and will not be later, full of smooth and tranquil waters; I can expect that there will be crisis in my life. Help me Lord to be spiritually focused and controlled during a time of crisis. Help me to continue to learn and know more about You, even if I don't feel very spiritually motivated. Protect the state of my mind and my tendency to reason on my own to solve my own problem. Help me to know that the answer is coming from You, and that I am discerning Your will. OH Lord, help me to focus more on You and in Your Word, and be transformed by the renewing of my mind—and recognize Your will. Father, I want to do everything that is good and acceptable and perfect; I want to be the new person that You want me to be!

▶▶ **Add now your own personal prayer.**

WHERE TO FIND ADDITIONAL HELP:
1 Thessalonians 5:23; Galatians 1:15.

Be listening for His advice

Live a life of faith. Be very attentive to God's voice so that you may be able to rely on Him to make the choices for you. God will transform the natural into the supernatural through your obedience to His voice. You must be willing to waive your rights and let God make your choice for you.

> *Is not the whole land before you? Let's part company.*
> *If you go to the left, I'll go to the right;*
> *if you go to the right, I'll go to the left.*
> —GENESIS 13:9

My oldest grandson, Justin, told me about the first Sunday school class he can remember. It was about Jesus' disciples being afraid, and asking Jesus to help them. Justin was talking about an account in the Bible that most people would remember as Jesus calming the storm. As a five-year-old, Justin was more impressed with the disciples' concerns, their faith, and their interest in seeking Jesus' advice.

The story appears in three of the Gospels. Here is how it reads in Matthew 8:23-27, "Then he got into the boat and his disciples followed him. Without warning, a furious storm came up on the lake, so that the waves swept over the boat. But Jesus was sleeping. The disciples went and woke him, saying, "Lord, save us! We're going to drown!" He replied, "You of little faith, why are you so afraid?" Then he got up and rebuked the winds and the waves, and it was completely calm. The men were amazed and asked, "What kind of man is this? Even the winds and the waves obey him!""

In the midst of my personal crisis, I can relate to a similar wind-gusting, wave-building, and boat-drenching storm. The disciples were afraid for their lives and thought they might drown, so they called on Jesus. They went to their Lord. They wanted to listen to what Jesus would say in the midst of their storm. They were seeking His advice. They were ready to be obedient to His voice.

JUMP-START PRAYER:
Abba, help me to continue to grow spiritually by adopting the discipline of waiving my rights, and letting You make the choice for me. God, I recognize that this goes against all of the teachings of this world that values individuality and personal choices; that is why this is so difficult, but I know that in You and with You, anything is possible. Lord, I recognize that this is the

difference between making good decisions by me Vs. Making excellent decisions through You. Help me to place my personal rights in the closet of my life, and to waive my right to choose; You choose for me! Help me to trust You, and then watch the results of Your excellent choice.

▶▶ **Add now your own personal prayer.**

WHERE TO FIND ADDITIONAL HELP:
Colossians 3:3; Matthew 16:24.

STEP 5

HOW YOU CAN BE CERTAIN TO HEAR GOD'S DIRECTIONS

Let your spirit connect to the life of Jesus

Be certain that God will reveal things in accordance with His will. If you have trusted Him as your personal Savior, you have begun the most significant, fulfilling relationship that you can experience. The sure promises of God provide confidence that Jesus lives in you and that He will never leave you. Let your spiritual nature be willing to submit to the life of Jesus, so that your understanding will be perfectly clear-because the Lord will make you one with Him.

> *In that day you will no longer ask me anything.*
> *I tell you the truth, my Father will give you*
> *whatever you ask in my name.*
> —John 16:23

How can we get our spirit to connect to the life of Jesus? Ephesians 3:16 reads, "I pray that out of his glorious riches he may strengthen you with power through his Spirit in your inner being," or in other words, to be strengthened with might through His Spirit.

Our "inner being" is who we are inside; it is our spiritual DNA, a new creation inside of our flesh, and our true identity. On the outside, we may still look exactly the same, our body build is identical, our gender remains the same, and our ethnicity is still the same, but on the inside we are a whole new person. It's the Spirit of God living in us that enables us to live a brand new life in Christ Jesus.

Our "inner being" can then be strengthened, and thereby connected to Jesus in the same way that we enjoyed the work of the Holy Spirit in our salvation. When He came to us, regenerated us, indwelled us, and sealed us. As we enjoyed His work in our behalf at our salvation, now we can enjoy His contemporary work-the work of the Holy

Spirit in our Christian life.

What a great promise! The Spirit of God is praying for us. The Spirit of God is guiding us, He is convicting us, He is teaching us through the Bible, He is sanctifying us, and He is filling us. God's Spirit in us will enable us to live a life that pleases Him.

JUMP-START PRAYER:
Abba, Father, thank You for Your promise that if I am willing to submit to the life of Jesus, one day I will be one with Him, and I will no longer have any questions. Thank You that Your Spirit in me enables me to live a brand new life in Jesus Christ. Father, I place myself at the foot of Your Cross. I abandon myself totally to Your life, and to Your control. Lord, let there be no distance between You and I, so that my understanding will be totally clear.

▶▶ **Add now your own personal prayer.**

WHERE TO FIND ADDITIONAL HELP:
Matthew 18:3; Mark 4:34; Revelation 3:20.

Ask God to reveal to you His "heart and mind"

In the midst of your crisis, ask God to reveal to you His heart and mind. Surrender yourself totally to God, so that you can "reach unity in the faith and in the knowledge of the Son of God and become mature, attaining to the full measure of the fullness of Christ." Aim to be lifted by God into the heavenly places through the baptism of the Holy Spirit, so that He can disclose to you His teachings-Then you can glorify Him!

> *In that day you will ask in my name.*
> *I am not saying that I will ask the Father on your behalf.*
> *No, the Father himself loves you because you have loved me*
> *and have believed that I came from God.*
> —JOHN 16:26, 27

As I read the Book of Acts, I discovered that the early church depended on prayer. They believed the promises of God and asked God for what they needed. In my sadness, I had forgotten that the purpose of Bible study is not simply to understand profound truths, but to get to know the Father better. The more I get to know God, the more confident I feel that I can ask Him to reveal His "heart and mind" to me.

Sometimes we may know more about God and His Word and work than we do about Him personally, it's like researching our favorite movie star. If we read everything written about him or her by studying their lives, habits, culture, and language; know about their families and careers. Then we will understand who they are. But even with all we've learned, it's still not personal. We've never met them, shared a meal, or spent time talking, laughing, crying—all the things that reveal the real person. It's refreshing to know that in our walk with the Lord, we can get to know Him in a personal way that makes us familiar with Him personally!

We need to read God's Book to find out how He wants us to run our affairs. A person makes decisions based on intelligence and morality, but He will show us that He is aware of what is right and what is wrong, what is good and what is evil. Romans 11:33-34 says, "Oh the depth of the riches both of the wisdom and knowledge of God!" Right now, in the midst of our crisis, is the perfect time for us to get to know Him better, to seek His advice, and to partake of His counsel.

JUMP-START PRAYER:
My Abba and my King, it is so difficult for me to keep my eyes on you when I am in the midst of a crisis. I always find myself

taking my eyes off the spiritual and placing my attention in the natural world. Lord, lift me up into the heavenly places, and help me to walk in the Spirit. Teach me and encourage me to surrender myself to You more and more each day, so that I can attain to the whole measure of the fullness of Christ. Please reveal to me your heart and mind. May Your Holy Spirit disclose to me your teachings and your wisdom, so that You may be glorified through my life.

▶▶ Add now your own personal prayer.

WHERE TO FIND ADDITIONAL HELP:
James 1:5; Proverbs 3:5-6; John 16:23; Psalm 73:24-25

Meditate on His Word and listen for His soft voice

Give God time to speak to you; meditate on His Word, and listen to His soft whisper. Feel His gentle hand guide you in your everyday choices. If He gives you a sense of doubt or restraint, stop at once and don't try to reason it out; God guides our common sense.

> *The LORD confides in those who fear him;*
> *he makes his covenant known to them.*
> —PSALM 25:14

A good friend, the Honorable Patrick A. White, who is the first African-American, United States Magistrate Judge for the Southern District of Florida, recently shared with me that in every case before him the toughest and most agonizing part of his job is the struggle to make the right and fair decision. Judge White's solution is to have a disciplined time of solitude and quiet time to study the case, and to hear God's soft voice by meditating in His Word. I won't take me by surprise to hear that Judge White ended up in the Supreme Court!

Psalm 119:15 says, "I mediate on your precepts, and consider your ways". That means to me: recalling what we've committed to memory and then turning it over in our minds to see the fullest implications and applications of the truth. That's what meditation is-recalling what we've put into our brain, and then turning it over and over in our minds. We want to see the fullest implications, and we want to see the applications. As we meditate on the Word of God, we're going to hear His sense of restraint and find out things to rejoice about. There is no doubt then, that a disciplined time of reading God's Scriptures will develop foundations that we can build in our work, our families, and on every-day living.

Every time I remember Judge White's words, I pray, "God help me to have the same kind of attitude." I believe that as I put effort into it, and I turn to God with that kind of heart's desire, He's going to hear and answer that prayer and help me develop a love for His Word.

JUMP-START PRAYER:
My Abba and my King, help me to protect my everyday time with You when I can find direction in your Scriptures, and can hear Your soft whisper, which gives me gentle guidance and direction. Lord, thank you for loving me so much. You are continually guiding me by producing doubt or restraint, or encouraging me by my everyday choices. Help me to heed Your instructions and allow You to guide my common sense.

▶▶| Add now your own personal prayer.

WHERE TO FIND ADDITIONAL HELP:
Mark 6:50; John 10:27; Joshua 1:8; Isaiah 1:8

www.ingramcontent.com/pod-product-compliance
Lightning Source LLC
Chambersburg PA
CBHW051957290426
44110CB00015B/2279